# Heaven's Guidebook
# to
# HOMEmaking
## A Look at Our Future Helps Our Home Today

## Janet Willis

*Heaven's Guidebook to HOMEmaking*
*A Look at our Future Helps Our Home Today*
©2019 Janet Willis
All Rights Reserved

Illustrations and Cover Design by Janet Willis

All emphasis of bold print is the author's.
## scottandjanetwillis.com

ISBN-9781688737211

Khesed Publications
Ashland City, TN

I wish to thank
the ladies of Parkwood Baptist Church
in Chicago, Illinois
who years ago helped me with this project.
As a marvelous mixture of young wives, mothers,
singles, widows, and older women,
we put our heads and hearts together
to gather verses and ideas
and expand on this theme.

# CONTENTS

## Our Goal: Make Our Home...

# Introduction

Wouldn't it be great if there was a home that was truly happy, one that you could look at as a perfect example to follow? Thankfully, there is! You can even take a virtual tour of this model home. And it's real. It's no dream. Best of all, you can be born into this family! It then becomes part of your inheritance. That's because it belongs to your Father, your Father Who is in Heaven. He built a very special home for you because He has plans for you, plans to give you hope and a future (Jeremiah 29:11).

You probably already heard about this home, its famous gates of pearl and streets of gold. And God's promise to wipe away all tears has brought tender comfort to many hurting hearts (Revelation 21:4). Often it's said we won't be able to imagine it, but that's not true. "What no eye has seen, nor ear heard, nor the heart of man imagined, what God has prepared for those who love Him, these things God has revealed to us through the Spirit" (I Corinthians 2:9-10, ESV). The last part of that verse is often missed. Things that we could not have imagined on our own **have** been revealed to us! And it is far more than most people realize.

No, we won't float on a cloud, playing a harp. That image evaporates when we delve into what God actually reveals. If we search God's Word carefully, we will see many characteristics about our Father's home that become an amazingly relevant guide for us in our own homes today. In other words, God's promises for our future can give us practical help for here and now. A focus on heaven provides help that is down to earth. Contrary to popular belief, being more heavenly minded **can** help us be more earthly good.

God not only has plans for your future, He also has a plan for your life right now. He does not leave us to flounder and guess. Not only that, but He gives clear direction specifically to women. The Bible says: "Older women...are to...encourage the young women to love their husband, to love their children, to be sensible, pure, workers at home" (Titus 2:3-5). Since I passed seventy a while back, I realized that verse is addressed to me. And if you are any younger than that, it relates to you. So, permit me to encourage you in these things. Love your family deeply, each of those family members God has graciously given you. Along with that, be sensible or self-controlled and be pure. Then God specifically mentions our domain: homemaking. Sure, we can delegate, but the responsibility has been given to us as women to see that necessary chores are done. Included in that job description are various skills such as cooking, organizing, and cleaning. When it comes to running the household, we are the CEO. Fortunately for us, there is an incredible array of devices and work savers to aid us in our task. And all kinds of print and online resources inspire and motivate us to be creative and efficient.

However, being a home maker can be so much more than that. We're not talking about simply keeping house but making a home. There is a difference. When we step inside this kind of dwelling we sense it immediately, whether it be the most humble of surroundings or the most elegant. Unfortunately, a truly sweet home like this is a rare find. In spite of all the advances in education and technology we enjoy, precious qualities often fall through the cracks. Treasured characteristics are forgotten. In our culture today, the word "home" has lost its draw, its magnetism, its value.

If we as women are to be keepers at home it might help to first stop and think why this has happened. What forces do we struggle against? What influences affect how we do **home** making? Think back to your childhood home. Shortcomings that may have existed in the home we grew up in sometimes influence the decisions we make. As we try to counter these weaknesses, we might lean too far in the other direction. Not only that, we might have blind spots that we are not even aware of. On top of all this, if we listen to the world around us, various philosophies swing us back and forth from one extreme to the other. Outside pressures literally push us in the direction of the latest current. However, we don't have to be a victim of our past. And we don't have to be a hostage of our culture.

Instead of looking to the expert of today, we can look to the expert of all time. God through His Word, gets us off that swinging pendulum and gives us balance. In the overwhelming sea of resources out there, the Bible is the one source we can trust. It is timeless. The technological benefits we enjoy today are no surprise to God. Neither are our problems. Dig into the treasure trove of His book. Ask God to open your mind and heart to any possible blind spots you might have as you press forward to fulfill your calling as a homemaker.

This guidebook will attempt to identify and help you study many specific characteristics that truly make a home sweet. The pages that follow cover thirty basic goals. Each goal originates from precious promises God gives us about our future home. Actually, these specifics about our future are more than promises. They are prophecies, guarantees from Almighty God: signed, sealed, and resting on His trustworthiness. Each prophecy is followed by related Bible references and practical suggestions to help us put that characteristic into practice in our home right now. Take your time thinking through each goal or characteristic. If you read one a day you will be done in a month. Each topic is touched on briefly, and so much more could be said. These entries might be a springboard for further discussion in your own circle of friends. Or best of all, some of the topics might help launch your own in depth Bible study. At the end of each chapter is a place for you to record your thoughts, things you want to remember, or things you want to study further.

Focusing individually on each of these prophecies helps us grasp in a greater way the lovingkindness of God. They reveal His understanding of our deepest needs. He already knows all about you, and as you go through this study, hopefully you will get to know God better. That is the key that unlocks potential for real change.

Now please understand that I'm not saying that a happy home is totally up to the woman. But by God's grace, with His strength, guided by His Word we can do our part, working toward making our homes a better place. As we allow Christ to rule and reign in our hearts, we will discover...

Anywhere
with Jesus
will be
Home
Sweet
Home

# #1

## A Place Where
# God Is Honored
# Above All

## Our Future Home

Every four years the Olympic opening extravaganza tries to outdo the previous one. But that is nothing compared to what we will experience in heaven. The apostle John testifies to us what he saw. Three different scenes seem to escalate in waves and they are breathtaking. John first portrays four mysterious creatures called cherubim along with 24 elders who say, "Worthy are You, our Lord and our God, to receive glory and honor" (Revelation 4:11). John's next scene makes us feel like we're in a virtual reality simulator: "I heard the voice of many angels around the throne and the living creatures and the elders; and the number of them was myriads of myriads, and thousands of thousands...and every created thing which is in heaven and on the earth and under the earth and on the sea, and all things in them [say], 'To Him who sits on the throne and to the Lamb, be blessing and honor'" (Revelation 5:11-13). But best of all in chapter seven, no more mere watching. We are in heaven ourselves, joining this multitude with our own voices! John says, "Behold, a great multitude which no one could count from every nation and all tribes and peoples and tongues, [are] standing before the throne and before the Lamb [saying], 'Blessing and...honor...be to our God forever and ever'" (Revelation 7:12). What a picture! For all eternity, the King of Kings, and Lord of Lords will be honored.

# Our Home Today

Now take a deep breath, come back down to earth, and picture what it's like in our country today. What does the word "honor" really mean? We stand to honor a judge when he enters a courtroom. It's a token of honor, an outward thing. But someone in that courtroom could be "sitting down" on the inside. God says sometimes His people "draw near with their words and honor Me with their lip service, but remove their hearts far from Me" (Isaiah 29:13). In other words, God knows our heart if we're "sitting down" on the inside! Honor for God must be genuine, a heart attitude, a state of mind. Do we understand and accept who God is? He is not only perfect (holy), but He is the **only** one who is perfect! "For You alone are holy" (Revelation 15:4) He must be first, we can have no other gods (Exodus 20:3).

What does that look like? How does that play out in our homes today? The Bible gives examples that test our hearts: what we do with our money (Proverbs 3:9) and what we do with our time (Isaiah 58:13). Once we lived on the second floor of a two flat (as they say in Chicago). We had no idea our first floor neighbors were peering out their window every Sunday watching our whole family come out the front door dressed up, Bibles in hand, as we piled in the car to go to church. Years later after we had moved, they told us about this and how God used it to bring them to the Lord. God helped us put Him first on the first day of the week, and eventually our neighbors did the same.

Early in our own walk with Christ, we saw how other families had ways to honor God in their homes. We saw how they put Scripture verses up around the house. We knew reminders would help us keep Him first in our hearts. Store bought and professional is beautiful and effective, but homemade can be precious. God's Words keep our focus on Who God is.

## My Thoughts

_____

_____

_____

_____

_____

_____

_____

_____

_____

_____

"You shall have no other gods
before Me."
Exodus 20:3

#2

# A Place with
# the Presence
# of Someone
# Special

## Our Future Home

The Bible gives an amazing promise to those who are Christians. Someday our Father's house, the New Jerusalem will come down and be here on earth. "I saw the holy city, new Jerusalem, coming down out of heaven from God...and I heard a loud voice from the throne saying, 'Behold, the dwelling place of God is with man, He will dwell with them, and....God Himself will be with them'" (Revelation 21:3, ESV). Not only that, but we will see His face (Revelation 22:4). He is not just **willing** to live with us, but that has been His plan all along, a close permanent fellowship with His people.

## Our Home Today

How we need the presence of God in our homes today! His presence is vital. We can ask for Him to come and rule in our hearts, and He will come! The Lord Jesus said, "Behold, I stand at the door and knock; if anyone hears My voice and opens the door, I will come in to him and will dine with him, and he with Me" (Revelation 3:20). He will let us know He is with us in countless ways. He convicts us when we need correcting and when we ask for His help, He graciously enables us to do right. His presence is a blessing both ways and so needed.

As I think back to my own mother, her presence was special. I am so grateful for her. She stayed at home to raise six children. Mom gave us not only quality time but quantity time. I realize not every woman growing up has had this blessing. Mom was a very hard worker and was always there for us. Home and Mom just went together.

Now, if I look in the mirror at my own life, I know as a wife and a mother my presence in my home ought to be be special to the members of my family. But my presence is only special if I stay right with God. And I know that is only possible if I lean on His strength. The Bible tells me that God's grace is sufficient. It says, "God is able to make all grace abound to you, so that having all sufficiency in all things at all times, you may abound in every good work" (II Corinthians 9:8). That takes away every excuse I could ever come up with!

I also realize the presence of others can **become** special. They actually become special by how I treat them. First and foremost this includes every member of my family. And by extension, it includes everyone who comes under my roof. I think particularly of reunions and holidays, when extended family and friends come over. The Lord reminds me to pray that these opportunities won't be squandered. "Look carefully then how you walk, not as unwise but as wise, making the best use of the time, because the days are evil" (Ephesians 5:15-16). When people gather together in my home, it is easy to get focused on media, entertainment, and gadgets. But people matter. Just think, many of the relationships we now have will continue on in eternity, and everyone will be lovable, then!

For now, we need to work at those relationships, and appreciate the presence of others. God says we should be "diligent to preserve the unity of the Spirit in the bond of peace" (Ephesians 4:3). Leaning on God's grace, we can "love one another earnestly from a pure heart" (I Peter 1:22, ESV).

# My Thoughts

_____

_____

_____

_____

_____

_____

_____

_____

_____

_____

_____

_____

"Behold, the dwelling place of God
is with man, He will dwell with them,
and ... God Himself will be with them"

Revelation 21:3, ESV

#3

# A Place of
# Comfort

A Place of
# Comfort

## Our Future Home

Someday in our heavenly Father's home our earthly sorrows will be gone, fully healed through God's personal comfort. God doesn't just tell us that He will provide comfort. He gives us a vivid picture of the kind of comfort He will provide, and He does that through a beautiful comparison. Just like a tiny babe is cradled in the arms of his mother and lovingly nourished, so will God comfort us in the New Jerusalem. "You shall nurse, you shall be carried upon her hip and bounced upon her knees, as one whom his mother comforts, so I will comfort you; and you shall be comforted in Jerusalem" (Isaiah 66:11-13 ESV). What a gracious heavenly Father we have who chose to use a picture of motherhood to portray His own tender comfort. We know that "He will wipe away every tear from [our] eyes; and there will no longer be any death; there will no longer be any mourning, or crying, or pain" (Revelation 21:4).

## Our Home Today

As I think of the comfort our heavenly Father will provide it reminds me of a time when I was a little girl. I was terrified by delirium from a fever and I vividly remember how my father comforted me. He held me tight and strong, gently patting me on the head, over and over reassuring me that he would not leave me. When I became an adult, I learned about the difficult childhood he had.

Many years later when he was 89 years old, I asked him how he ever learned kindness since he grew up under foster care that was cruel and harsh. He told me there was a dear old lady that his foster family would go to visit, "Aunt Frances." She was kind to my father and treated him like he was special.

God tells us that we should comfort one another with the comfort He has given us (II Corinthians 1:4). My dad did that. Somewhere along his journey growing up, he chose to not get bitter or wallow in self-pity about what he experienced in his own childhood home. Instead he chose to follow Aunt Frances' example, and oh how I benefitted from his wise choice!

Years ago, our married daughter Amy came to visit. She sat next to me nursing our first grandchild. I was nursing my eighth baby, Elizabeth, Amy's only sister (after six boys in a row!). What a blessed experience it was for both of us to be able to comfort our babies through nursing!

Then three and a half years later, I experienced the hardest trial of my life. Not only little Elizabeth, but six of my children were killed in a van accident. Allow me to pass on to you, the comfort God gave me.

Hours after the accident, the thought came to me, 'It was all a waste!' My hands were burned and I could not pick up my Bible, but a verse quickly came to mind: "Your labor is not in vain in the Lord" (I Corinthians 15:58, KJV). That was the first Bible verse I ever memorized. The whole chapter talks about Christ's resurrection and the new bodies God has promised us. I would see my children again. The long view made all the difference (Psalm 73). Eternity will last a whole lot longer than this life!

Tears of sorrow were not wrong. I missed my kids terribly. But tears of bitterness and self-pity would only complicate my grief. I grieved, but not as those who have no hope (I Thessalonians 4:13-18). God's truth was vital and my greatest comfort!

## My Thoughts

_____

_____

_____

_____

_____

_____

_____

_____

_____

_____

_____

"God...comforts us in all our affliction
so that we will be able to comfort
those who are in any affliction
with the comfort with which we ourselves
are comforted by God."

II Corinthians 1:4

#4
# A Place Where
# Visitors
# Are
# Welcome

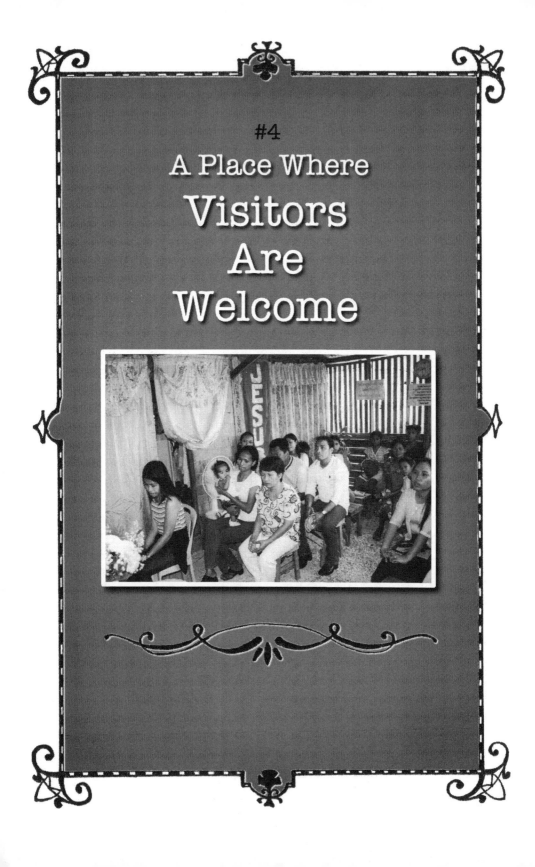

A Place Where
Visitors Are Welcome

## Our Future Home

What a stunning welcome God gives to us! It's a picture that draws us in. The gates of the New Jerusalem are always open! "Your gates will be open continually; they will not be closed day or night" (Isaiah 60:11, cf. Revelation 21:25). Jesus, the ultimate gracious Host says, "I go to prepare a place for you" (John 14:2). The invitations abound. "Come, everyone who thirsts, come to the waters" (Isaiah 55:1, ESV). The Bible's final chapter includes the word "come" three times (Revelation 22:17). Not everyone responds to this invitation, but everyone is invited, the welcome has been published and proclaimed.*

## Our Home Today

We are encouraged in Scripture to practice hospitality. "Be hospitable to one another without complaint" (I Peter 4:9) (see also Romans 12:13). And how do we do that? We can follow our Lord's example and prepare a place for others to feel at home in our home.

Nowadays there are so many new convenient ways to connect with people. Social media has benefits. But the drawback is that messages darting back and forth in cyberspace are fragmented. In depth conversations are rare. Even Face Time cannot fully compete with the extended actual live presence of a person. People are complex.

In our first few months of belonging to a Bible believing church my husband and I were invited into the homes of several families. We saw Christianity in action. The folks were not afraid to be transparent. They were unselfish in sharing what they had and made us feel accepted, even special.

We can make others feel special when they see that we have prepared ahead of time for their visit. On the other hand we want our guests to feel relaxed so they can enjoy themselves. Balance is important. Remember Martha who was cumbered about with much serving (Luke 10:40), maybe making hospitality more complicated than it needed to be. It doesn't have to be fancy; sometimes just a sandwich or a cup of cold water will do! The important thing is creating a welcoming atmosphere. If we overdo and get weary sharing our home, we end up not doing it very often. And Jesus encouraged us with an amazing promise: those that give that simple cup, God will reward (Matthew 10:40).

I will never forget years ago when my husband and I walked through a shanty town outside of Manila in the Philippines. It was teaming with people in dire poverty and their only way to make a living was to scavenge a nearby garbage dump for whatever would sell. Bathrooms were non-existent and people filled their water buckets from a common source. Constructed from whatever scraps a person could find, the homes gave little privacy or comfort. Yet, a woman cleaned and cleared a space in her shack to set up a few benches. She hung a bright homemade banner and held Bible studies for her neighbors. That welcome not only bore fruit in the changed lives around her, but it was an example to this American woman of what hospitality is all about: loving people, loving your neighbor.

*The way to accept this astounding invitation is to accept the fact that Jesus alone paid our way by dying on the cross. "As many as received Him (Jesus Christ) to them He gave the right to become children of God, even to those who believe in His name" (John 1:12).

## My Thoughts

_____

_____

_____

_____

_____

_____

_____

_____

_____

"Be hospitable to one another
without complaint."
I Peter 4:9

#5

A Place of

# Hugs and Affection

# A Place of
# Hugs and Affection

## Our Future Home

Around dinnertime when our van pulled up outside, our four younger boys used to leap and jump around wildly saying, "Dad's home! Dad's home!" I can picture that moment when someday my husband arrives in heaven. Imagine the hugs, the tears, the kisses! Our Lord Jesus put that love in our hearts for our children and we are trusting His promise for that reunion to come!

How do we know hugs will be in heaven? We have read what Jesus did when he was here on this earth. "They were bringing children to Him so that He might touch them; but the disciples rebuked them. When Jesus saw this, He was indignant and said to them, 'Permit the children to come to Me; do not hinder them; for the kingdom of God belongs to such as these....And He took them in His arms and began blessing them, laying His hands on them" (Mark 10:13-16).

## Our Home Today

In our lives today, God gives us a powerful exhortation: "Love one another with a pure heart fervently" (I Peter 1:22, KJV). In addition, He provides us many precious word pictures of how that kind of love played out in real life. Past hurts were forgiven as we see Esau running to meet his brother Jacob. Esau "embraced him, and fell on his neck and kissed him, and they wept" (Genesis 33:4).

Many years later, Jacob learned his son was alive after years of thinking he had been dead. As soon as Joseph "appeared before him, he fell on his neck and wept on his neck a long time" (Genesis 46:29). Ruth "clings" to her mother-in-law Naomi as she says, "Do not urge me to leave you...for where you go, I will go....Your God [shall be] my God" (Ruth 1:14-17). Jesus tells of a father's affection for his prodigal son who had come home. "While he was still a long way off, his father saw him and felt compassion for him, and ran and embraced him and kissed him" (Luke 15:20). Friends of Paul knew they might not see him again this side of heaven. They "began to weep aloud and embraced Paul, and repeatedly kissed him" (Acts 20:37).

Affection can be a beautiful outward display of God-like love. Touching another human being certainly seems to be encouraged in Scripture. But Scripture also gives us some warnings. Love "does not seek its own" (I Corinthians 13:5). There must be balance and sensitivity to the other person's feelings. "Sexual immorality and all impurity or covetousness must not even be named among you, as is proper among saints" (Ephesians 5:3). It is interesting that covetousness is included in this context. Holy affection is pure and selfless. It is first of all considerate of the other person and takes into account cultural customs. For instance, when Paul says "greet one another with a holy kiss" (Romans 16:16), we might have to make some adaptations to what might be normally accepted in our community.

Now if you are a wife or a mother, remember the advice Titus gave that was discussed previously: love your husband and love your children (Titus 2:4). The Greek word for "love" in this passage points toward wholesome physical affection. For some people, this all comes naturally, but to others they need to work at it. Of course, what God says is what really matters, but it is interesting that even some scientific evidence says our emotional and physical health can benefit from physical human contact! So go ahead, give those heavenly hugs!

## My Thoughts

_____

_____

_____

_____

_____

_____

_____

_____

_____

_____

_____

Jesus "took them in His arms and began blessing them, laying His hands on them"
Mark 10:16

#6

A Place
of
Order

## Our Future Home

Sometimes people wonder what we will do in the future when our Father's home is here on earth. What will eternal life really be like? God says we will rule and reign with Him for the first thousand years of the Kingdom (Revelation 20:4). It's amazing how many details about this time period are revealed yet are often glossed over and ignored. Some specifics might not pertain to us directly, but they give us hints at the type of life we will enjoy. For believers, life will have a divine purpose and structure. God already gave the plans He has for the layout of His capital city and its surroundings. The mortal descendants of Levi and Zadok will live in special neighborhoods near the Temple and some of their duties are explained in detail (Ezekiel 48:9-12). Believe it or not, even traffic control going to and from the Temple is delineated (Ezekiel 46:9). Talk about order! Ezekiel says a special city lies south of the Temple (Ezekiel 40:2). And he gives the names and locations of each gate (Ezekiel 48:30-34). This is the New Jerusalem, home for immortals whose names are written in the Lamb's book of life (Revelation 20:21-27). Just like our cities today, these gate names help the residents find their way around. "Hey, I'll meet you just inside the Judah gate!"

# Our Home Today

When Moses was given the task of making an earthly dwelling place for God, the directions were explicit. "See... that you make all things according to the pattern which was shown you on the mountain" (Hebrews 8:5). God instructed. It was not haphazard, but rather like the old adage, 'A place for everything, and everything in its place.' God gave the plan and Moses faithfully executed that plan.

When it came to my own home, it was up to me to forge a plan, to think ahead, to make the best possible use of the resources I had available, to be the "home" maker. When we lived in small places, I asked God for ideas how to make every nook and cranny count. If I found some tasks overwhelming, I prayed for His help to even get motivated. Sometimes my prayer request was simply for energy. Sometimes the need of the hour was getting my priorities right!

As my family grew, I quickly learned (often the hard way) that organization was the way of peace! I learned later that is a Biblical principle. "God is not the author of confusion, but of peace" (I Corinthians 14:33, KJV). It prevented countless irritations, frustrating minutes trying to find things. I saved cardboard boxes of all shapes and sizes and recycled them into drawer and closet organizers. And they were free!

When Israel was in the wilderness, God also gave instructions about cleanliness. Keeping our home clean was good for the health and safety of my family. I learned after the experience of many moves that packing up an entire household was a great motivator to simplify and declutter. At the next house, it made cleaning easier!

Being on time is also part of an orderly life. The good habits of my husband eventually transformed my bad habits of running late. Promptness shows consideration for others. I still struggle with planning ahead, especially with meals, although I do prepare ahead for Sunday. I appreciate the principle of gathering the manna (Exodus 16:22-30). A day of rest helps me launch an orderly new week. It's like hitting the refresh key!

## My Thoughts

_____

_____

_____

_____

_____

_____

_____

_____

_____

_____

"All things must be done properly
and in an orderly manner."
I Corinthians 14:40

# A Place of
# Beauty

A Place of
# Beauty

## Our Future Home

"And I saw the holy city, New Jerusalem, coming down out of heaven from God, made ready as a bride adorned for her husband" (Revelation 21:2). Around the world nearly every culture can understand this word picture. Traditions might vary but they usually agree the wedding day is one day in a girl's life when she should look her very best. And the adornment of God's city is the pinnacle of artistry. "Out of Zion, the perfection of beauty, God has shown forth" (Psalm 50:2). John says, "The city was pure gold, like clear glass" (Revelation 21:18). Isaiah speaks of the future Jerusalem and tells of jewels (Isaiah 54:11-12), perfect lighting (Isaiah 60:19), and the natural beauty of wood (Isaiah 60:13). John describes trees that flower and bear fruit (Revelation 22:2). God's home is real and it will be our home!

## Our Home Today

So how does this apply to my home today, you wonder? We haven't seen His city yet, so how can we even guess what God's version of beauty will look like? Actually, there are clues throughout the Bible. God provided detailed patterns for the Tabernacle (Exodus 25:8-9) and the Temple (I Chronicles 28:11, 19). God's architecture from the past teaches principles of design. For a clue on furniture arrangement, we can analyze the Creator's work in nature. Divide a tree down the middle.

It's not symmetrical, yet somehow the "weight" is balanced. For an interesting color clue, notice the background God chose for all His multi-colored flowers. Forest green or leaf green seems to "go" with everything. Speaking of green, maybe add houseplants or silk greenery. Notice the city is made of gold, a color that is warm and cheerful (Revelation 21:18). We see that lighting is important (Isaiah 60:19), so open the curtains and let the sun shine in. In the evening, strategically place those lamps. Our Father's creative work reveals principles that guide us.

I have to personally confess that as an artist, I love beauty but I had to keep my budget in mind. I struggled with covetousness in my early years, and had to pray to God to learn contentment. I asked Him for ideas that I could afford. He is the only true Creative One, and He said, "In the hearts of all who are skillful I have put skill" (Exodus 31:6). So I asked Him for skill to make my home a place of beauty with the resources I had. I also needed to be sensitive to my husband's wishes and my family's needs. My home had to be inviting and livable!

Years ago, God helped get me through the long drawn out renovation of our home. Our bargain priced house inspired the neighbor kids to ask our boys if we lived in a haunted house! My husband worked on the exterior as well as the interior, but he also worked two jobs at this point. I knew I would be facing the raw drywall for some time, so I cheered up the living room with my kid's drawings matted on colored paper. The kitchen had no cabinets, but I used the existing one long shelf to hold some crates I had. I borrowed an idea from a local bakery and decorated the crates with paper doilies. It only cost me a dollar! Eventually, by God's grace, the neighbors said our house was one of the nicest houses on the block, and I truly thanked the Lord, my Advisor, my Sustainer, and my Decorator!

# My Thoughts

"Out of Zion, the perfection of beauty,
God has shown forth."

Psalm 50:2

#8

# A Place Where
# Important Work
# Is Accomplished

## Our Future Home

Very few people can say that they love their job. Thus, for most people the word "work" brings negative thoughts. We long for weekends when we can rest, have pleasure, and relax. Someday when we are home with the Lord, we will surely have all these things. But we are also told His bond-servants will serve Him (Revelation 22:3). All work is not punishment. After all, some work was assigned to Adam before the Fall. "The LORD God took the man and put him into the garden of Eden to cultivate it and keep it" (Genesis 2:15). At that point sin had not entered the world. Serving God was a genuine joy, and someday, it will again be a delight. From the very core of our being, our hearts will be dedicated to the service of God. One of God's prophets reveals a fascinating detail of life in the Kingdom. Not just people but things will be set apart, dedicated to the Lord. "Every cooking pot in Jerusalem and Judah will be holy to the LORD of hosts" (Zechariah 14:21).

## Our Home Today

Have you ever been so excited working on a project that you didn't even want to stop to eat? Our work in heaven might be just like that. Jesus told his disciples, "My food is to do the will of Him who sent Me and to accomplish his work" (John 4:34). These days most of us have many tasks on our "to do list" that are not exactly our favorite thing to do. We often find ourselves in circumstances beyond our control, pulled in many directions. God gives guidelines to help us evaluate what our priorities ought to be. He says the virtuous woman is committed to her home, her family. Her diligence reveals where her heart is. "She looks well to the ways of her household, and does not eat the bread of idleness" (Proverbs 31:27). This involves sacrifice. "She rises also while it is still night and gives food to her household and portions to her maidens" (Proverbs 31:15).

Wonderful promises encourage us that this is worthy work. "Therefore, my beloved brethren, be steadfast, immovable, always abounding in the work of the Lord, knowing that your labor is not in vain in the Lord" (I Corinthians 15:58). God is watching you clean up after your sick child in the middle of the night. This is real love and it is "through love [that we] serve one another" (Galatians 5:13).

My flesh is weak and I imagine yours is too. We can ask God to help us love like we ought to love. I have found it to be a real battle to change my attitude and actions. But God encourages us in that battle. "Whatever you do, do your work heartily, as for the Lord rather than for men, knowing that from the Lord you will receive the reward of the inheritance" (Colossians 3:23-24).

We have the Lord Jesus for our example of what it means to serve others, "for the Son of Man did not come to be served, but to serve, and to give His life a ransom for many" (Matthew 20:28). One wonders if there is anything that could top that. But I believe there is. The glorified Lord of heaven will actually gird Himself to serve, and have [us] recline at the table, and will come up and wait on [us] (Luke 12:37). Though this will occur in our future home, I wanted to conclude with it here. This is the God we serve!

# My Thoughts

"She looks well to the ways of her household and does not eat the bread of idleness."

Proverbs 31:27

#9

# A Place Where
# Needs Are
# Satisfied

## Our Future Home

Satisfying needs seems to be on everyone's mind these days. God gives us this marvelous promise about our future: "I am the Alpha and the Omega, the beginning and the end. I will give to the one who thirsts from the spring of the water of life without cost" (Revelation 21:6). In our future home, God will supply not only our physical needs but also our emotional needs as well. "Happiness and joy will overwhelm them" (Isaiah 51:11, NET).

## Our Home Today

When I was a busy mom, I knew it was up to me to meet many needs that my family had. Feeding my family could be a duty to endure or an opportunity to bless the ones I love. Occasionally when pressures mounted, it was all right to lean on substitutes to meet a few of those needs: pop a convenient frozen dinner in the microwave, put on a video for the kids, or get a sitter for a night out.

But when it came to certain needs that my husband had, substitutes would not do. Now God clearly puts the responsibility on men to beware of the adulterous woman who can lure him into sin (Proverbs 5; 6:23-35; 7:6-27). But we wives can also learn from these Scriptures. After all, we are told to "be wise as serpents and harmless as doves" (Matthew 10:16). We can prepare our appearance and creatively arrange our bedroom. A little mystery and variety can spice things up. Show initiative. If at all possible, meet him at the door. Encourage him and build him up. Look him in the eye and be genuinely interested in what he has to say. "Who can find a virtuous woman? For her price is far above rubies. The heart of her husband doth safely trust in her, so that he shall have no need of spoil" (Proverbs 31:10-11, KJV).

You might be thinking, "But what about **my** needs?" An interesting verse addresses that. "Do not merely look out for your own personal interests, but also for the interests of others" (Philippians 2:4). At first glance this verse warns us to beware of selfishness, of thinking only of our own needs. But note the word "also". God is not saying we should think **only** of the other person's needs. This passage actually demonstrates a critical balance. And that principle of balance can have implications for our intimate relationship.

God has a wonderful design for mutual pleasure for both the husband and the wife. Some have called it the "super glue" of marriage. Surprisingly explicit, God gives guidance in this (I Corinthians 7:3-6). In fact, a whole book of the Bible, the Song of Solomon, is devoted to this subject showing how both physical and emotional needs matter. It is a goal we can pray for in the here and now in our relationship.

But you might say, my husband and I aren't there yet. Pray and ask God to help you obtain and then retain that sweet mutual intimacy. It's alright. After all, it was God's idea in the first place! "For this reason a man shall leave his father and his mother, and be joined to his wife; and they shall become one flesh" (Genesis 2:24). Remember the advice given earlier: "encourage the young women to love their husbands" (Titus 2:4). The original language of those last three words is one word: "philandros". It means: have a warm affection toward your man!

46

# My Thoughts

"Do not merely look out
for your own personal interests,
but also for the interests of others."
Philippians 2:4

# #10

# A Place of
# Understanding
## and
# Being Understood

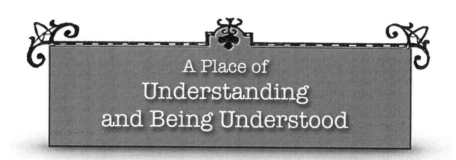

## Our Future Home

The Bible describes the future of believers like this: "Now we see in a mirror dimly, but then face to face; now I know in part, but then I will know fully just as I also have been fully known" (I Corinthians 13:12). Job had this confidence: "Even after my skin is destroyed, yet from my flesh I shall see God; whom I myself shall behold, and whom my eyes will see and not another" (Job 19:26-27). We will know God as He now knows us. What an amazing truth! Someday in our Father's home, we will see Him just as He is (I John 3:2). Questions that puzzle us now will then be clear and understood.

## Our Home Today

Sometimes our present relationships at home can get frustrating when we are misunderstood. When our sincerity is doubted, others assume they know our heart; or when we are misjudged, we get discouraged and even angry. And of course we can be on the flip side of that problem. We sometimes misjudge others.

As much as we want to be understood, we need to be willing to work at understanding others. For some people opening up is very difficult. Asking good questions might help. It shows that you care. On the other hand, we must not pry open the door of their heart. Maybe showing that you are focused on their virtues will help them to trust. The apostle Paul says, "Finally, brethren, whatever is true, whatever is honorable, whatever is right, whatever is pure, whatever is lovely, whatever is of good repute, if there is any excellence, and if anything worthy of praise, dwell on these things" (Philippians 4:8). Understanding someone takes time. It takes sensitivity and even patience. God gives us advice in this area. "Be swift to hear, slow to speak" (James 1:19). An important part of loving others includes being a careful listener. Turn off the device, or any extra noise. Look into their eyes. With little children, get down on their level. As long as there is no emergency, resist the temptation to hurry them up. As they grow, the busyness of life can crowd out sweet moments when they might want to confide in us. Sometimes we just need to slow down.

My mom and dad were good listeners. And that helped me now as an adult to believe that God actually is willing to listen to me! I can trust that my prayers don't bounce off the ceiling. I can trust that He understands me, even if no one else does. David wrote, "O LORD, You have searched me and known me. You know when I sit down and when I rise up; You understand my thought from afar. You scrutinize my path and my lying down, and are intimately acquainted with all my ways. …Such knowledge is too wonderful for me; it is too high, I cannot attain to it" (Psalm 139:1-9).

Most important of all, we must seek to know the Lord and then grow in our understanding of Him. "That [we] may know Him and the power of His resurrection and the fellowship of His sufferings, being conformed to His death; in order that I may attain to the resurrection from the dead" (Philippians 3:10-11). God says, "Let not a wise man boast of his wisdom…but let him who boasts boast of this, that he understands and knows Me, that I am the LORD who exercises lovingkindness, justice, and righteousness on earth; for I delight in these things" (Jeremiah 9:23-24).

## My Thoughts

_____

_____

_____

_____

_____

_____

_____

_____

_____

_____

_____

"Be swift to hear,
slow to speak."
James 1:19

# #11

# A Place of
# Joy

# A Place of Joy

## Our Future Home

Someday we will "shout for joy on the height of Zion....[We will] be radiant over the bounty of the LORD." Our life "will be like a watered garden, and [we] will never languish again" (Jeremiah 31:12). We will come to Mount Zion and actually live in the city of the living God (Hebrews 12:22-24). In His presence we will experience the "fullness of joy" (Psalm 16:11). Why did our God even make this city? "Behold, I create Jerusalem for rejoicing And her people for gladness" (Isaiah 65:18). The context here is the Jerusalem of the future. God's own words declare His love for us and reveal His goodness. It's His gracious plan to give us joy!

## Our Home Today

So how can we get some of this joy in our home right now? The Bible talks about joy a lot and says some things that might surprise you. To begin with, it is not an option. We are told to "Rejoice in the Lord **always**" (Philippians 4:4). Amazing! We're not only commanded to have joy, but to have it all the time! So how do we obey that? Let's look back at what else Paul says. He went through incredible trials and said he had "no rest". He was tormented by "conflicts without, (and) fears within". Then he says, "I am overflowing with joy in all (my) affliction" (II Corinthians 7:4-5). This sounds like a contradiction, almost an absurdity. But hundreds of years earlier, an Old Testament prophet declared the same thing.

Though his crops had failed and his source of income had vanished, he declared: "Yet will I rejoice in the LORD" (Habakuk 3:17).

Maybe we need to unpack all this. What is joy anyway? Is joy a feeling that just happens? What is the source of real joy? And how do we get it? We must look carefully at what is imbedded in these phrases from Scripture. The words "in the LORD" are critical. Our circumstances change, but the LORD never changes. Therefore, we can choose to rejoice in Who God is... always.

Imagine three train cars, labeled: feelings, faith, and facts. Which one should be the engine? Are you driven by your emotions or by truth? Knowing and understanding God's Word should be first. Then we can choose to accept God's Word, putting our faith in it. "Faith comes from hearing, and hearing by the Word of Christ" (Romans 10:17). Then feelings will follow that faith. In other words, deep seated genuine joy is the result of getting right with God. So joy is a result, a fruit of the Spirit (Galatians 5:22).

Personally, when I work around the house and spontaneously sing to the Lord, it's because I'm keeping the train engine up front. "I will sing with the Spirit, and I will sing with the mind also" (I Corinthians 14:15). Truths from the Bible occupy my mind, are accepted by faith, and rejoicing bursts forth! I just have to work on the "always" part! I need God's help to faithfully "walk in the Spirit" like Paul and Habakuk. (Galatians 5:16). About 2400 years ago, Nehemiah told the Israelites, "The joy of the LORD is your strength." It was time "to celebrate...**because** they understood **the words** which had been made known to them." They heard God's Word, responded with humility and repentance, and now it was time to rejoice (Nehemiah 8:10-12). Oh, and notice that joy was "of the LORD." It was grounded in the unchangeable God. Hallelujah!

# My Thoughts

"Rejoice in the Lord always"
Philippians 4:4

# 12

# A Place Where
# Children
# Are Welcome

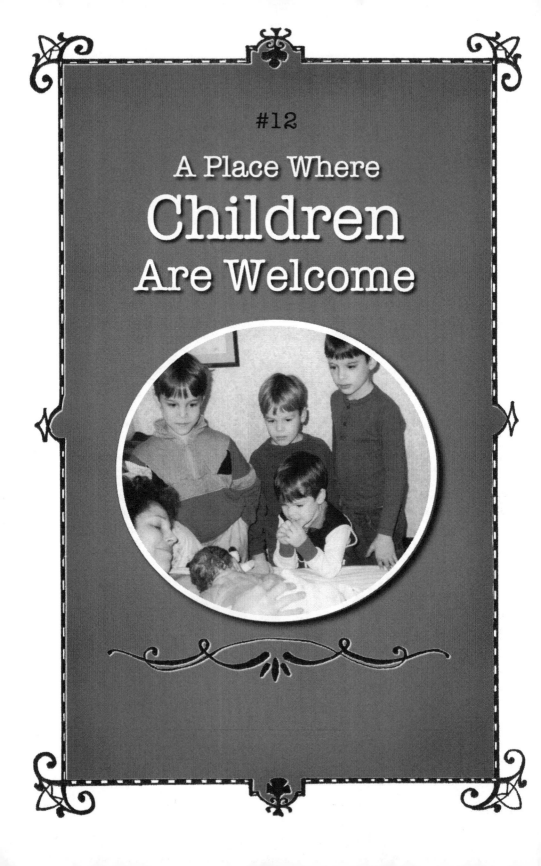

A Place Where
Children Are Welcome

## Our Future Home

Many people wonder, "Are there children in heaven?" Other questions arise: Do people who die when they are babies or children remain as they were forever? Do they gradually grow up in heaven? Will we all be 20 or 30 years old when we get our resurrection bodies? God graciously gives us so much information about our future, but He chose to not reveal specific answers to these questions. But we are given hints of what heaven will be like because of our Lord's example while He was here on earth. Jesus picked up little children and held them. He strongly rebuked those who thought children were a bother. He blessed little ones and laid His hands on them (Mark 10:15). What we can say for certain is that children are very precious to our heavenly Father. Jesus said, "Let the children alone, and do not hinder them from coming to Me; for the kingdom of heaven belongs to such as these" (Matthew 19:14).

## Our Home Today

From the beginning, when God created people, He said, "Be fruitful and multiply, and fill the earth" (Genesis 1:27). It was a mandate. Furthermore, He told us that children were His gift to us. "Children are a gift of the Lord, the fruit of the womb is a reward" (Psalm 127:3). Even if we are not able to have children ourselves or if we no longer have children living in our home, we can make our home a place where children are welcome.

I'll never forget how Grandma Willis just had a small apartment, but saw to it that she had crayons and paper, and a bag of toy soldiers for my boys. My own mother and dad made their many grandchildren feel welcome by bringing out a bin full of games, and for the holiday dinner Dad made a low table to fit some small chairs he bought. A footstool was by the bathroom sink. When possible, breakable knick-knacks were temporarily placed high so as not to unnecessarily tempt my toddler's hands. That's simply following God's example of being considerate and kind. After all, God only gave Adam and Eve one "no" in the garden!

Interestingly, today public places have become more inviting to children. Stores and even airports often have a "kid's corner." We did this in our church's fellowship hall. When pot luck dinners were over, children could go to a "play corner" with a rug, a few carefully chosen toys, and comfy chairs so moms could continue to fellowship with one another. It helped families to stick around and mingle and really get to know each other.

Even in our sanctuary, we used office dividers with plexiglass on top, to section off a "nursery" that made it possible for mothers to still be "in" the worship service. Toddlers were free to move about in a contained area. A few quiet baby toys were there along with rocking chairs. A nursery worker was available to help if a mom needed a hand. The mothers loved it! Maybe even more important, little ones at their most impressionable age became accustomed to seeing families worshipping together.

When we make our homes and our churches child-friendly, they become a little taste of heaven. Jesus made this clear. He taught us just how we are to value each child, raising the bar almost beyond comprehension. "Whoever receives one such child in My name receives Me" (Matthew 18:5).

## My Thoughts

_____

_____

_____

_____

_____

_____

_____

_____

_____

_____

> "Children are a gift of the Lord, the fruit of the womb is a reward."
> Psalm 127:3

#13

A Place
of
Rest

# A Place of Rest

## Our Future Home

God has promised a future rest for His people, giving details of a very real existence here on earth. David said, "Rest in the LORD and wait patiently for Him…those who wait for the LORD, they will inherit the land" (Psalm 37:7-9). David mentions this land inheritance six times in that psalm! Moreover he says, "the righteous will inherit the land and dwell in it forever" (Psalm 37:29).

This permanent promise of land was first given unconditionally to Abraham (Genesis 15). Those who have trusted in God's Messiah, Jesus, are grafted in to that amazing promise. "If you belong to Christ, then you are Abraham's descendants, heirs according to promise" (Galatians 3:29, see also Romans 11:1–24).

This place of rest, the promised land in Israel is where God's city will be. "For the LORD has chosen Zion; He has desired it for His habitation. This is My resting place forever; here I will dwell, for I have desired it" (Psalm 132:13-14; Ezekiel 40:2 and 48:30-35; Revelation 21:10-13).

We can rest in the Lord now, trusting His promise of a future rest. And what is that future rest? Our biggest battle, our struggles with sin will be over, forever!

## Our Home Today

That is the reason our home today isn't exactly heaven on earth. We aren't perfected yet, and neither are the members of our household. We each battle our own sin nature (Romans 7:18-25). No wonder homes and hearts get broken!

But Jesus said, "Come to Me, all who are weary and heavy-laden, and I will give you rest. Take My yoke upon you and learn from Me, for I am gentle and humble in heart, and you will find rest for your souls. For My yoke is easy and My burden is light" (Matthew 11:28-30). We find rest for our souls when we trust in His work. He died for us and paid the penalty for our sin. From the cross, He called out, "It is finished!" (John 19:30). That term actually means "paid in full." If we understand, repent, and put our faith in Him, our account is settled. That is the rest we can enjoy right now in the present, knowing our sin price has been paid. But best of all, we can look forward to an eternal rest in our Father's Kingdom.

Years ago, when I was a busy mom, I often did not think of the word "rest" in spiritual terms. My older three were grown and gone and my days were packed homeschooling four young boys. With another baby on the way, rest meant getting some much needed sleep. Then I came across this. "It is in vain that you rise up early and go late to rest, eating the bread of anxious toil; for he gives to his beloved sleep" (Psalm 127:2, ESV). There was that principle of balance again. I had a tendency to lay awake worrying. I understood the privilege I had to teach and train little ones. The stakes were high. I wanted them to be with me forever in God's Kingdom, in that promised land. I knew there was a battle for their souls and I as a mother had the opportunity to spend the most time with them in their critical early years. I had to prioritize my work day, pray, and rest in the LORD. Then each night I could pillow my head and sleep! His yoke was easy, His burden was light. It was a full time job, but a joyous job.

# My Thoughts

"My yoke is easy,
and My burden is light."
Matthew 11:30

#14

# A Place of
# Praise

A Place of
Praise

## Our Future Home

Throughout the book of Revelation, praise to God is not given in generalities. The "whys" are spelled out. He is the Creator (4:11). His works are great and marvelous and He alone is holy (15:3-4). The Lamb, God the Son, gave His life for us (5:12). Just listen to the celebration when God sets up His Kingdom: "I heard something like a loud voice of a great multitude in heaven, saying, "Hallelujah! Salvation and glory and power belong to our God." Again we hear the "whys": "...because His judgments are true and righteous" (Revelation 19:1-2).

When we arrive in the Kingdom we will be praising God for Who He is. But praise will even come **from** Him to those who have been steadfast. How precious it will be if we hear His "well done, good and faithful servant" (Matthew 25:21). And praise will be more than verbal. God says "every man shall receive his own reward according to his own labor" (I Corinthians 3:8). Here again specifics will matter. "For we must all appear before the judgment seat of Christ, that each one may receive what is due him for the things done while in the body, whether good or bad" (II Corinthians 5:10). It matters how believers live! Crowns will be given! "Do you not know that in a race all the runners run, but only one gets the prize? Run in such a way as to get the prize. Everyone who competes in the games goes into strict training. They do it to get a crown that will not last; but we do it to get a crown that will last forever" (1 Corinthians 9:24–25). Ultimately, all praise will go to God when crowns are laid at His feet (Revelation 4:9-11). It is His strength that enables us to do any good!

# Our Home Today

But we are still here, so does the Bible guide us now? Definitely! Patterns of praise fill the pages of Scripture. Study the divinely inspired lyrics. When the Psalmist says,"His praise shall continually be in my mouth" (Psalm 34:1), he goes on to give many "whys". Because He is kind and good, He heard my prayers, He delivered me from my fears, He was near to me when I was broken-hearted. Some psalms praise God by giving a detailed replay of historical events, how God has worked in the past.

These patterns guide us in how to edify our own family. We can "encourage one another and build up one another" by recounting the specific good we see in them (I Thessalonians 5:11). If you have children, you can "catch" them doing something good. Give specifics, yes, but keep it balanced. All good gifts come from God. "In the hearts of all who are skillful I have put skill" (Exodus 31:6). Learning to tie a bow was a big deal for my little Hank, but I also wanted him to be grateful to God for his new found ability. I wrote on his homemade paper crown "I know how to tie a bow. Thank you Jesus, for helping me grow." Today's culture makes pride a virtue, but the Bible teaches otherwise. We must not listen to the king of pride, for his eventual demise is sure.

Even our word choice matters, especially today when definitions are in a continual flux. Once my husband was asked by a waiter, "Would you like mashed potatoes or french fries?" Scott answered, "Fries." "Awesome!" the waiter replied. Awesome? Really? Maybe at least that word should be reserved for the Almighty!

# My Thoughts

"Encourage one another,
and build up one another."
I Thessalonians 5:11

# #15

# A Place of
# Safety

# A Place of Safety

## Our Future Home

God tells us that the New Jerusalem will someday be on earth and it will be a place of safety, a place where we will be secure. "The wolf shall dwell with the lamb, and the leopard shall lie down with the young goat…and a little child shall lead them. The cow and the bear shall graze; their young shall lie down together; and the lion shall eat straw like the ox. The nursing child shall play over the hole of the cobra, and the weaned child shall put his hand on the adder's den. They shall not hurt or destroy in all my holy mountain" (Isaiah 11:6-9, ESV). It is a protected and well-guarded place. The city has "a great and high wall, with twelve gates, and at the gates twelve angels" (Revelation 21:12). God tells us that "nothing unclean, and no one who practices abomination and lying, shall ever come into it" (Revelation 21:27).

## Our Home Today

Our home should be a safe haven for all who come under our roof. When it comes to children, Jesus gave a profound and stern warning. Calling a child out from the midst of the crowd, and placing him where all could see, Jesus said, "Whoever receives one such child in My name receives Me; but whoever causes one of these little ones who believe in Me to stumble, it would be better for him to have a heavy millstone hung around his neck, and to be drowned in the depth of the sea" (Matthew 18:5-6). This admonition could also be applied to how we care for anyone whose abilities are less than ours, such as the disabled and the elderly.

Just like any other mom, I knew many a sleepless night when patience wore thin, and my body was weary. Truths from the Scriptures came to mind: "See that you do not despise one of these little ones, for I say to you that their angels in heaven continually see the face of My Father who is in heaven" (Matthew 18:10). I knew what was right. Step away in another room to cool down, and pray. When I had none of my own patience left, God helped me. And God will help you. By His strength we can control our temper. With His help we can control our words and our actions. God says that a virtuous wife will have the law of kindness in her tongue (Proverbs 31:26). Whatever it takes, our home should be a place of safety. And as a preventative measure, we need to take care of ourselves physically. We owe it to our children. For their sake we need to eat sensibly and take that nap even though our 'to do' list is calling to us.

Also as a mother, we should be vigilant protecting our children from evil influences that might creep into our home, harmful influences from our culture that come through electronic devices and the various media. We can set the rules, for ourselves and for them. "I will walk within my house in the integrity of my heart. I will set no worthless thing before my eyes" (Psalm 101:2-3). Our children will meet temptation eventually, but we must protect them even while we strengthen them to be prepared to face the outside world.

"Do not be conformed to this world, but be transformed by the renewing of your mind. Then you will be able to discern what is the good, pleasing, and perfect will of God" (Romans 12:2). God's Word transforms and protects!

# My Thoughts

_____

_____

_____

_____

_____

_____

_____

_____

_____

_____

_____

_____

_____

"The teaching of kindness
is on her tongue."

Proverbs 31:26

#16

# A Place of
# Music

## A Place of
# Music

## Our Future Home

Music will be a magnificent part of our future. A massive choir in heaven will raise their voices in song before God's very throne. "And they sang...'Great and marvelous are Your works, O Lord our God, the Almighty; righteous and true are Your ways, King of the Nations!'" (Revelation 15:3) What a thrill to our ears and hearts that will be! Someday we will have the privilege to have a part in that heavenly choir. Not only that, but there are instruments in heaven, people are holding harps and angels are blowing trumpets (Revelation 5:8; 8:6). "Glorious things are spoken of you, O city of God...those who sing as well as those who play the flutes shall say, 'All my springs of joy are in you'" (Psalm 87:3-7).

## Our Home Today

In our homes we can practice for those future concerts and praise God through music right now in the present. In fact, that is one of the evidences of being Spirit-filled, and it's not an option, but a command! "Be filled with the Spirit, speaking to one another in psalms and hymns and spiritual songs, singing and making melody with your heart to the Lord" (Ephesians 5:18-19).

We often sang together as a family in our home, in our car, and in our church. My husband had us sing acappella in four part harmony, something that is quickly becoming a lost art. Learning his part didn't come easy for him. He had to work at it, plunking out his part on the piano. But what a blessing! The apostle Peter says, "all of you be harmonious, sympathetic, brotherly, kindhearted, and humble in spirit" (I Peter 3:8). If we apply this to music, it involves diversity within a unity, different parts working together as whole. None of us had great voices, but we learned to sing on pitch. Singing together in our little family assemble forced us to listen carefully to each other (sympathetic) and work as a unit (harmonious). Our family needed to have a brotherly, kindhearted, humble attitude to accomplish this. And we certainly needed God's help with that!

During his reign, King David, a harpist himself, greatly expanded the music program in his kingdom. "Four thousand were praising the LORD with the instruments which David made for giving praise" (I Chronicles 23:5). At special times, everyone got involved! "David and all Israel were celebrating before God with all their might, even with songs and with lyres, harps, tambourines, cymbals and with trumpets" (I Chronicles 13:8). Congregational heart felt music is a powerful blessing!

God has supplied a whole collection of lyrics in the largest book of the Bible for our example. Giving us only lyrics leaves freedom for a variety of styles. After all, someday we will see believers from all nations of the world throughout history singing to the Lord at His throne. The Psalms include the entire breath of human emotions in honest frankness, yet the ultimate goal is to communicate God's truth. "Let the word of Christ richly dwell within you, with all wisdom, teaching and admonishing one another with psalms and hymns and spiritual songs, singing with thankfulness in your hearts to God" (Colossians 3:16).

I thank the Lord for my mom, an excellent piano teacher, who gave lessons to our children. She also encouraged us to have the children listen to quality music even as infants and toddlers. It was ear training, she said. Who knows, the blessings of musical education might not just last a lifetime, but might last throughout eternity!

## My Thoughts

_____

_____

_____

_____

_____

_____

_____

_____

_____

"Let the Word of Christ
richly dwell within you...
singing with thankfulness
in your hearts to God."
Colossians 3:16

#17

A Place
of

# Tender
# Mercy

# A Place of Tender Mercy

## Our Future Home

When we come to live in God's city, just imagine what life will be like. It will be easy to love our neighbors because all our neighbors will be lovable! And wonder of wonders, we will be lovable too! How precious will be His forgiveness, His tender mercy for all eternity. God's prophets have spelled out what He does with our sin. He will "have compassion on us; He will tread our iniquities under foot. Yes, [He] will cast all [our] sins into the depths of the sea" (Micah 7:19). He will remove our transgressions "as far as the east is from the west" (Psalm 103:12), and He will remember them no more (Jeremiah 31:34).

## Our Home Today

In your own community, do you have trouble loving your neighbor? How about loving those under your own roof? God says we should be merciful toward one another. "Be kind to one another, tender-hearted, forgiving each other, just as God in Christ also has forgiven you" (Ephesians 4:32). This verse is loaded. It points back to God as our example. Forgiving is hard enough, but forgetting? How is that humanly possible?

I learned the first clue to forgiving was to examine my own heart. I'll never forget the first time I really saw God's measure or standard. "You are to be perfect, as your heavenly Father is perfect" (Matthew 5:48). Suddenly what I thought was a sliver of a sin in my life was really a log in

God's eyes! It made me look at the people around me in a different way. Jesus said, "How can you say to your brother, 'Let me take the speck out of your eye,' and behold, the log is in your own eye? You hypocrite, first take the log out of your own eye, and then you will see clearly to take the speck out of your brother's eye" (Matthew 7:1-5). To get the true perspective, I had to look at myself through God's magnifying glass. When I recognized how serious it was to offend a holy God, and how desperately I needed God's tender mercy, it helped me be careful about judging others. "He who is forgiven little, loves little" (Luke 7:47), and the one who is forgiven much, loves much.

That was the first step, but there was more. I am to forgive like God forgives, and He forgives only when a person repents (Acts 3:19). Even from the cross, Christ didn't forgive those who tortured Him. He prayed that the Father would forgive them (Luke 23:34). What if my family member is not sorry? I can pray for them and have a readiness to forgive, just like Jesus. "Never take your own revenge, beloved, but leave room for the wrath of God, for it is written, 'Vengeance is mine, I will repay,' says the Lord. But if your enemy is hungry, feed him, and if he is thirsty, give him a drink....Do not be overcome by evil, but overcome evil with good" (Romans 12:17-21). Kindness can display a readiness to forgive. And, more importantly, it displays God's readiness to forgive! I need to be careful not to allow bitterness to take root (Hebrews 12:15), but trust God's Holy Spirit to convict.

And when apologies do come, no matter how many times, I must still forgive (Matthew 18:21-22), and yes, even forget. Love "keeps no record of wrongs" (I Corinthians 13:5, NIV). With God's help, I can choose to focus on their virtues (Philippians 4:8).

# My Thoughts

"Be kind to one another; tender-hearted,
forgiving each other,
just as God in Christ
also has forgiven you."
Ephesians 4:32

# 18

# A Place Where Hearts Are Humble

A Place Where
Hearts Are Humble

## Our Future Home

Jesus "called a child to Himself and set him before them, and said, 'Truly I say to you, unless you are converted and become like children, you will not enter the kingdom of heaven. Whoever then humbles himself as this child, he is the greatest in the kingdom of heaven'" (Matthew 18:2-4). In other words, to enter God's kingdom and reside in His house, humility is required! Just picture it. A spirit of humility will prevail in the hearts of all who live in our Father's home. Relationships will be sweet and stay sweet!

## Our Home Today

But what exactly does Jesus mean using a child as an example of humility? Little children can be downright ornery and self-willed. Any mother can attest to that. The reality of their sin nature becomes evident to every parent early on. On the other hand, little children are also totally dependent on adults to take care of them. Jesus was saying that we must acknowledge our complete dependence upon God in order to enter His kingdom. Solomon said, "O LORD my God, You have made Your servant king in place of my father David, yet I am but a little child; I do not know how to go out or come in" (I Kings 3:7). This adult man who had just been given power over God's chosen people realized his place in God's grand plan. King Solomon recognized his position in relation to the King of the Universe and confessed his need to learn from the Almighty. Maybe that is part of what humility is: understanding our place, and therefore our need.

When we are around little children, we see this dependency played out. Two, three, and four year olds are moldable. They have a natural bent to learn. They often mimic the attitudes and mannerisms of the adults around them. They are not just teachable, but eager learners and carefully observant, like good scientists. As an experienced mother of nine, I must say my kids' accurate imitation of me was often very convicting. The "humility" of my children motivated me to be mindful how I responded to the stresses of life. I couldn't always say like the apostle Paul, "Be imitators of me, just as I also am of Christ" (I Corinthians 11:1).

Speaking of imitation, I think of Martha's sister, Mary. To me she is the perfect picture of a teachable dependent spirit. She sat at Jesus' feet to drink in His words. And He commended her. She had chosen "the good part" (Luke 10:42). King David prayed, "Teach me to do Your will, for You are my God" (Psalm 143:10). David and Mary humbled themselves before God. We can do that too when we open our Bible, pray, and listen to Him.

Now humbling ourselves before God is one thing, but there's more. "With humility of mind regard one another as more important than yourselves" (Philippians 2:3). Now that is **really** hard! Humility before a perfect God is one thing but humility before another sinner like myself? I might cringe at His command, yet I marvel at His example. "Have this attitude in yourselves which was also in Christ Jesus, who...did not regard equality with God a thing to be grasped, but...He humbled Himself by becoming obedient to the point of death, even death on a cross (Philippians 2:5-8). The Perfect humbled Himself. Why? For the imperfect, so we could enjoy His  sweet home someday. If we sit at His feet and ask for His help, we can have a taste of that sweet home now!

## My Thoughts

---

---

---

---

---

---

---

---

---

> "With humility of mind
> regard one another as more important
> than yourselves."
>
> Philippians 2:3

#19

# A Place of
# Belonging

## Our Future Home

Jesus Christ gives believers a fascinating promise. "He who overcomes...I will write on him the name of My God, and the name of the city of My God, the new Jerusalem, which comes down out of heaven from My God" (Revelation 3:12). We will be permanently connected, a part of the most grand and glorious plan ever devised. We will belong.

Don't miss the apostle John's first century time travel account. He saw this New Jerusalem descending out of heaven. He "heard a loud voice from the throne, saying, 'Behold, the tabernacle of God is among men, and He will dwell among them, and they shall be His people, and God Himself will be among them'" (Revelation 21:3). We will belong somewhere! His city will be our changeless enduring home. But best of all, we will belong to God. We will be His people.

## Our Home Today

What about today? Are there any practical ways that we as homemakers can help our families have a little earthly taste of belonging? We might try to encourage family traditions. Sometimes this just happens naturally. Family t-shirts, family photo walls, and photo albums all foster a team spirit. We can decorate our house with our own family's homemade things and children's artwork. It's very interesting that when you want to sell a house, realtors advise you to get out all personal touches like this because potential buyers have a hard time "picturing" themselves in your house. It must be pretty powerful, this business of being a HOMEmaker!

However, God has far more important ways to give us a sense of belonging. I remember many years ago, I read a gospel tract. Alone in my bedroom I prayed and asked Christ to forgive me and be my Savior. Jesus, the Good Shepherd brought me into His fold. "My sheep hear My voice, and I know them, and they follow Me; and I give eternal life to them, and they will never perish; and no one will snatch them out of My hand. My Father, who has given them to Me, is greater than all; and no one is able to snatch them out of the Father's hand. I and the Father are one" (John 10:27-30).

Unfortunately, for several years I floundered and did not grow as a Christian. God's plan for Christians is to connect with one another in local churches. He says to "not [neglect] to meet together, as is the habit of some, but [encourage] one another, and all the more as you see the Day drawing near" (Hebrews 10:25). Eventually I realized I needed to ask God to direct me where He wanted me to go. He definitely did! We joined a good Bible-believing church, and soon were attending all their services. It wasn't long before we got involved serving, and that really tied us together with our church family, a bond that was precious. "So we, who are many, are one body in Christ, and individually members one of another" (Romans 12:5).

Our church had a Sunday school program of going through the whole Bible chronologically in three years. Learning the stories of believers who had lived thousands of years before gave us the big picture, God's epic, of which we are a part. We learned a deep appreciation for the Jewish roots of our faith. And reading the biographies of Christians who lived over the last two thousand years has been vital. God has worked down through history connecting us all and enriching us with His ownership. We are His!

## My Thoughts

---

---

---

---

---

---

---

---

---

---

---

"My sheep hear My voice,
and I know them, and they follow Me...
no one will snatch them out of My hand."
John 10:27

#20

A Place
Where
Help Is
Available

### Our Future Home

"The city of the living God, the heavenly Jerusalem" is home to thousands upon thousands of angels (Hebrews 12:22). They are "ministering spirits, sent out to render service for the sake of those who will inherit salvation" (Hebrews 1:14). They are God's helpers, invisible to us, but very real and faithful to their assigned tasks.

When this Jerusalem descends, it will be the capital city of God's Kingdom on earth. The Jerusalem that is now above will someday come down (Galatians 4:26; Revelation 21:2). From this home base, resurrected believers will be sent out with assigned tasks to rule and reign with Christ (Revelation 20:6). Thus, both now and in the future, God's home is a place where help is available.

However, the ultimate source of aid is our all powerful God. He makes the decisions, the assignments. He "is our refuge and strength, a very present help in trouble" (Psalm 46:1). David was thanking God for His help and wrote, "I was crying to the LORD with my voice, and He answered me from His holy mountain....I will not be afraid of ten thousands of people who have set themselves against me round about" (Psalm 3:4-7).

### Our Home Today

God promises to help us here in our homes and in our families when we call upon Him. "Fear not, for I am with you; be not dismayed, for I am your God; I will strengthen you, I will help you, I will uphold you with my righteous right hand" (Isaiah 41:10, ESV). Time and time again, when I have been discouraged, verses I memorized come back to me: "Why are you in despair, O my soul? And why have you become disturbed within me? Hope in God, for I shall again praise Him for the help of His presence" (Psalm 42:5). "But as for me, I will watch expectantly for the LORD; I will wait for the God of my salvation. My God will hear me. Do not rejoice over me, O my enemy. Though I fall I will rise; Though I dwell in darkness, the LORD is a light for me" (Micah 7:7-8).

His help then supplies strength for me to help others. It's our assigned task to "bear one another's burdens" (Galatians 6:2). We can "strengthen the weak hands, and make firm the feeble knees. Say to those who have an anxious heart, 'Be strong; fear not!'" (Isaiah 35:3-4, ESV). We can help also through prayer. It is like a secret weapon for good. "When you pray, go into your inner room, close your door and pray to your Father who is in secret, and your Father who sees what is done in secret will reward you" (Matthew 6:6). The apostle Paul speaks of the armor of God and names two weapons, the Word of God and prayer. He says, "pray at all times in the Spirit, and with this in view, be on the alert with all perseverance and petition for all the saints" (Ephesians 6:18).

I know God helps me, and He can use me to help others, but I have to remember His conditions: Pray "in the Spirit." "To this one I will look, to him who is humble and contrite of spirit, and who trembles at My word" (Isaiah 66:2). God help me remember the "if's" in Your Word! "If you abide in Me, and My words abide in you, ask whatever you wish, and it will be done for you" (John 15:7).

# My Thoughts

"Bear one another's
burdens."
Galatians 6:2

#21

# A Place of
# Stability

# A Place of
## Stability

## Our Future Home

"God is our refuge and strength, a very present help in trouble. Therefore we will not fear, though the earth should change, and though the mountains slip into the heart of the sea; though its waters roar and foam, though the mountains quake at its swelling pride. Selah. There is a river whose streams make glad the city of God the holy dwelling places of the Most High. God is in the midst of her, she will not be moved" (Psalm 46:1-5). These are powerful words, flat out scary, yet ending with a beautiful hope. God's city will not be "moved," meaning "shaken." Our Father's house is stable, permanent, solid, sure! After all, its "builder and maker is God" (Hebrews 11:10). It is the city which is to come (Hebrews 13:14). It is the city that our eyes will someday behold. "Your eyes will see Jerusalem, an undisturbed habitation, a tent which will not be folded; its stakes will never be pulled up, nor any of its cords be torn apart" (Isaiah 33:20). We will "receive a kingdom which cannot be shaken" (Hebrews 12:28).

## Our Home Today

This last verse was a huge help to me, because we moved quite a bit. It was never a frivolous decision for us to move, but God directed and we were willing. But I do love thinking that for my last move, I won't have to pack a single box! Or unpack on the other side!

A move might seem like a great trial, but suffering far worse than that can happen. We don't know what a day may bring forth. We might not want to think about this, but it's true: troubles are inevitable, "as sure as the sparks fly upward" (Job 5:7). Life is messy in the middle. Andree Seu Peterson has a great article about this (*World Magazine*, May 26, 2007). She says, "Satan wants you to believe the middle will last forever." But it won't. "The woman with the 12 years of bleeding (Luke 8) and the man lame for 38 years (John 5)—these are stories short in the reading but long in the living. But see what Jesus brought about."

So what do we do in the meantime? Jesus painted this vivid picture: "Everyone who hears these words of Mine and acts on them, may be compared to a wise man who built his house on the rock....the rain fell, and the floods came, and the winds blew and slammed against that house; and yet it did not fail for it had been founded on the rock" (Matthew 7:24-25). Are gales slamming against your home, your family? Stay in God's Word. It will help you focus on who God is. He is all-powerful (in charge, on His throne) and He is good. Andree says, "God, like any good Father, sees around corners for His children and snatches them out of the way of oncoming cars. He also drags His kids, kicking and screaming, from their cherished mud puddles, to take them to the beach."

When storms slam into your world, God says, "Be still, and know that I am God" (Psalm 46:10, ESV). "I will be with you" (Isaiah 43:2). Trust Him…and keep the long view. "The sufferings of this present time are not worthy to be compared with the glory that is to be revealed to us." (Romans 8:18).

Your trust can be catchy. God might use you to help stabilize others in the family.

# My Thoughts

"Be still, and know
that I am God.
Psalm 46:10, ESV

#22

A
Place
of
Accountability
and
Justice

# A Place of Accountability and Justice

## Our Future Home

Someday every person who has ever lived will actually get to see God on His throne. What will that be like? We are warned: "Righteousness and justice are the foundation of Your throne" (Psalm 89:14). The apostle John was allowed to witness God's justice in the future: "And I saw the dead, small and great, stand before God; and the books were opened: and another book was opened, which is the book of life: and the dead were judged out of those things which were written in the books, according to their works....And whosoever was not found written in the book of life was cast into the lake of fire" (Revelation 20:12-15, KJV). The Bible informs us, "God will bring every act to judgment, everything which is hidden, whether it is good or evil" (Ecclesiastes 12:14). God's omniscience is not to be taken lightly. "Accordingly, whatever you have said in the dark will be heard in the light, and what you have whispered in the inner rooms will be proclaimed upon the housetops" (Luke 12:3).

## Our Home Today

Some say it's not loving to strike fear into people's hearts. But telling the whole truth about God can bring good. "The fear of the LORD is the beginning of wisdom" (Proverbs 9:10). I would never have appreciated God's mercy unless I first understood God's justice. It's that balance again. He provided a solution to my desperate condition because He delights to give mercy (Micah 7:18). I had to be willing to be accountable to God, take responsibility for my sin, and look to Him for forgiveness.

When I did that and trusted Christ as my Savior I was born again into God's family. God is now my Father, and He keeps me in line. "Those whom the LORD loves He disciplines" (Hebrews 12:6). He disciplines out of love and He has a purpose. "All discipline for the moment seems not to be joyful, but sorrowful; yet to those who have been trained by it, afterwards it yields the peaceful fruit of righteousness" (Hebrews 12:11).

When I had my own children, I saw how God wanted me to follow His example of loving discipline. "He who withholds his rod hates his son, But he who loves him disciplines him diligently" (Proverbs 13:24). It was the same principle, and had the same goal. It had to be consistent and measured, not done with a loss of temper. The goal is the peaceful fruit of righteousness! True love is active, not passive. Most babies learn to crawl the hard way. They quickly figure out how to put one hand forward, then the other hand, or else they bop their nose on the floor! They allow pain to train! So it is with God's discipline. "The rod and reproof give wisdom" (Proverbs 29:15). After I discipline my child, I can restore with a hug! We can then pray aloud together asking for God's help to do right next time.

God gives advice about other family relationships. "Confess your sins to one another, and pray for one another so that you may be healed" (James 5:16). An honest transparency demonstrates that we are willing to be accountable to one another. It can help build trust. God even gives advice on how to deal with someone who has offended you (Luke 17:3-4). Don't let accounts fester. "If possible, so far as it depends on you, be at peace with all men" (Romans 12:18). Sometimes we have to just leave it in God's hands. Ultimately, His justice will prevail.

# My Thoughts

_____

_____

_____

_____

_____

_____

_____

_____

_____

_____

_____

_____

"The fear of the Lord is the
beginning of wisdom."
Proverbs 9:10

#23

# A Place of
# Fun!

## A Place of Fun

### Our Future Home

Someday when we live in our Father's house, God will wipe away every tear. But even more than that, Jesus said, "Blessed are you who weep now, for you shall **laugh.** (Luke 6:21) His promises are over the top. God says we will be "like those who dream...our mouth [will be] filled with **laughter** and our tongue with joyful shouting" (Psalm 126:1-2). I love each picture He paints with His Word. "The streets of the city will be filled with boys and girls **playing** in its streets" (Zechariah 8:5). It actually sounds like fun! God says we "will go forth and **skip about** like calves from the stall" (Malachi 4:2). He specifically says in the New Jerusalem He will comfort us like a mother who bounces her baby on her knees (Isaiah 66:12-13). That Hebrew word for "bouncing" can mean sport or play! I bet you didn't know that heaven on earth would actually include fun!

### Our Home Today

Once I was reentering the United States after visiting a foreign country. There in the airport, something hit me that I will never forget. I was struck with the smiles, joking, and laughter around me. People who didn't even know each other were interacting in a friendly manner. I realized for the last twelve days I hadn't seen that. People were subdued. Smiles were missing. I felt the palpable contrast between oppression verses freedom. Oh, the blessed gift of freedom some countries enjoy! Yes there are times when we mourn but Solomon also said there is "a time to dance" (Ecclesiastes 3:4). I think of the video of Jewish people dancing in the street when Israel became a nation. King David danced before the ark as it was brought in to Jerusalem (II Samuel 6:14-15).

As we scan the whole of Scripture, we continue to see the wonderful principle of balance. After a particularly busy day for Jesus and His disciples, where "there were many people coming and going, and they did not even have time to eat" the Lord advised, "Come away by yourselves to a secluded place and rest a while" (Mark 6:31). I remember many a time as a mother when my first three were all little I did not have time to eat! Taking a break for a nap when they napped revived me. And taking time for recreation and fun was not just valuable, but critical. It's burnout prevention.

So what sounds like fun to you? Board games, whiffle ball, bike riding, telling riddles and jokes? When many of our grandchildren were teens, our son got the idea of a photo scavenger hunt in downtown Chicago. The old competitive spirit kicked in between the two teams and they had a crazy fun time! What does your family like to do together or individually? "A cheerful heart is good medicine" (Proverbs 17:22, NIV). Having some good clean fun renews the spirit. My husband has a marvelous gift of lighting up my life with his wit and humor. He also has a good sense for when it's time to take a break. He keeps my workaholic tendencies in balance.

Way back when we were kids, television was just getting underway and air conditioning was unheard of. Houses were hot in the summer so we played outside from sunup to sunset. With jumprope, softball, and kick the can, we were "boys and girls playing in the streets!" It was a little taste of heaven.

# My Thoughts

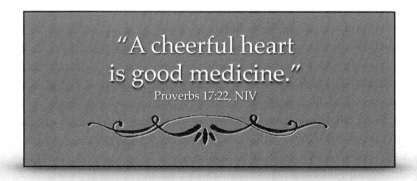

"A cheerful heart
is good medicine."
Proverbs 17:22, NIV

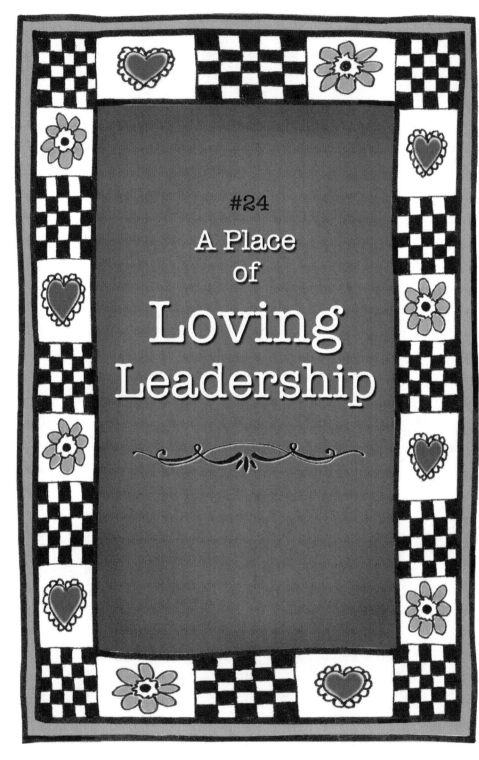

#24

A Place
of
Loving
Leadership

# A Place of Loving Leadership

## Our Future Home

God formed this planet to be inhabited (Isaiah 45:18). He says, "I am God, and there is no other; I am God, and there is no one like Me, declaring the end from the beginning....My purpose will be established, And I will accomplish all My good pleasure" (Isaiah 46:9-10). He told us how the battle began in Eden, and He told us how it will end (Genesis 3:15). Yes, even way back then. Someday His Messiah's Kingdom will come on this earth, and He will announce, "It is done" (Revelation 21:6).

He is in charge. That is leadership. But from the very first chapter in the Bible, we learn that His leadership is not just good, but very good (Genesis 1:31). That's just who He is. We can read that "God is love" (I John 4:8), but we also see His love in action through the history recorded in the Bible. And we will see that in the future. Strength is tempered with kindness. Our God "will come with might, with His arm ruling for Him....Like a shepherd He will tend His flock, in His arm He will gather the lambs and carry them in His bosom; He will gently lead the nursing ewes" (Isaiah 40:10-11). What a picture of loving leadership!

## Our Home Today

My husband's mother had a favorite saying, "Live and learn." She probably used that as a threat as she guided her son through his teen years! He eventually grew up, married me, then thankfully, became a Christian. He became an avid student of the Word, reversed that pattern, and began to learn and live. We both did. We learned God's plan for how families should function. Governments, companies, armies, and families all function best when there is one head, with supporting staff. As a wife and mother, I had to learn to let him lead, and he had to learn to lead in love. The Bible is always balanced. Fathers are cautioned, "do not provoke your children to anger, but bring them up in the discipline and instruction of the Lord" (Ephesians 6:4). And as a father, he encouraged our children to respect me. "Hear, my son, your father's instruction, and do not forsake your mother's teaching" (Proverbs 1:8). Little by little we learned the Bible and taught it to our children. We certainly didn't do it perfectly, but God's plan was to show a united front! God wanted us as parents to be loving leaders, filled with His Spirit showing "love, joy, peace, patience, kindness, goodness, faithfulness, gentleness, [and] self-control" (Galatians 5:22-23).

Throughout the Bible, we saw transformed lives of men and women who accomplished astounding feats of courage and faith. We also found leaders that were flawed. That's just real life, and the Bible is brutally frank. Some leaders were not just flawed, but evil, and some cultures were opposed to God. Abigail, Esther, Rahab, and Ruth dealt with difficult situations and can be examples to us as women. Joseph and David are examples to men.

Most importantly, the Bible puts on display the character of God. He is the only perfect example of loving leadership. Understanding His sovereignty and His love were anchors that helped me through the worst trials in my life (I Peter 4:12-13). The big picture and the long view of life is key! "And we know that all things work together for good to them that love God, to them who are the called according to his purpose" (Romans 8:28, KJV).

# My Thoughts

_____

_____

_____

_____

_____

_____

_____

_____

_____

_____

_____

_____

_____

"The fruit of the Spirit is love, joy,
peace, patience, kindness,
goodness, faithfulness, gentleness,
self-control"
Galatians 5:22-23

# 25

# A Place of
# Unity

A Place of
Unity

## Our Future Home

Our Father's home, the New Jerusalem, is described as a mountain throughout the Bible. God gives us word pictures of this, and I think He means what He says. It is most likely a pyramidal shaped structure that will be the largest and highest point on the earth during Christ's Kingdom. "Now it will come about that in the last days the mountain of the house of the LORD will be established as the chief of the mountains, and will be raised above the hills; and all the nations will stream to it. And many peoples will come and say, 'Come, let us go up to the mountain of the LORD, to the house of the God of Jacob; that He may teach us concerning His ways and that we may walk in His paths.' For the law will go forth from Zion and the word of the LORD from Jerusalem" (Isaiah 2:2-3). The prophet goes on to say that after God judges the nations, peace will ultimately reign. "And He will judge between the nations, and will render decisions for many peoples; and they will hammer their swords into plowshares and their spears into pruning hooks. Nation will not lift up sword against nation, and never again will they learn war" (Isaiah 2:4).

Our Father's Kingdom will come, His will will be done, on earth as it is in Heaven! And when He finishes His judgments, wars will be no more.

# Our Home Today

Our world is full of all kinds of conflict, from an angry war of words to cyber warfare to tragic physical harm. The outside world is not friendly to Biblical values. Sometimes this is hard, but we are encouraged, "If possible, so far as it depends on you, be at peace with all men" (Romans 12:18).

However first and foremost, our inside world, our home needs to be a place of unity. "Behold, how good and how pleasant it is for brothers to dwell together in unity!" (Psalm 133:1) God knows it won't be easy. We have to work at it and be "diligent to preserve the unity of the Spirit in the bond of peace" (Ephesians 4:3). It will be a powerful testimony back to the outside world. "By this all men will know that you are My disciples, if you have love for one another" (John 13:35). Jesus prayed for us to have the kind of unity He has with the Father. "The glory which You have given Me I have given to them, that they may be one, just as We are one; I in them and You in Me, that they may be perfected in unity, so that the world may know that You sent Me, and loved them, even as You have loved Me" (John 17:22-23). Again, a testimony to the outside world is vital: "so that the world may know."

Easier said than done, you are thinking! Here are just a few suggestions: "pursue the things which make for peace [by] the building up of one another" (Romans 14:19). Keep short accounts: "Be angry and yet do not sin; do not let the sun go down on your anger" (Ephesians 4:26). Watch our heart attitude: "Do all things without grumbling or disputing" (Philippians 2:14). And ladies, we need to guard our tongue: "It is better to live in a desert land than with a contentious and vexing woman" (Proverbs 21:19). Ask God for help and remember the perfect example of unity Jesus talked about: "that they may be one, just as We are one."

## My Thoughts

_____

_____

_____

_____

_____

_____

_____

_____

_____

_____

_____

"By this all men will know
that you are My disciples,
if you have love for one another."
John 13:35

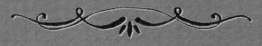

# 26

# A Place of
# Tranquility

A Place of
# Tranquility

## Our Future Home

"There is a river, whose streams make glad the city of God, the holy dwelling places of the most High" (Psalm 46:4-5). Being near a body of water is soothing. A lake, a river, or an ocean can have a calming effect on our mental state, our emotions. Present day Jerusalem has none of these anywhere close. But huge topographical changes will occur just before God sets up His Kingdom here on earth. This is why God's prophets paint a picture of the future Jerusalem that is very different. "Look upon Zion, the city of our appointed feasts....there the majestic One, the LORD, will be for us a place of rivers and wide canals on which no boat with oars will go, and on which no mighty ship will pass" (Isaiah 33:20-21). Small sailing vessels might be permitted which would make for a quiet, peaceful scene.

Now if we do a little treasure hunt and compare Scripture with Scripture, amazing details of an entire water supply system become evident. Living water will flow from the throne of God (Revelation 22:1) down throughout the New Jerusalem, then out to the Temple (Ezekiel 47:1). From the Temple it will flow both toward the East and the West (Zechariah 14:8), and even cleanse the Dead Sea (Ezekiel 47:8).

When Isaiah talks of Zion's rivers and wide canals, he includes a critical truth along with his prophesy: "the people who dwell there will be forgiven their iniquity" (Isaiah 33:24). We who live in our Father's home will have more than calmness, we will have a permanent peace in our soul, perfect tranquility!

# Our Home Today

So you might be thinking, until then tranquil moments are pretty rare in our home. God knows about your struggles and He actually has lots to say about the way to peace. "Be anxious for nothing but in everything by prayer and supplication with thanksgiving let your requests be made known to God. And the peace of God, which surpasses all comprehension, will guard your hearts and your minds in Christ Jesus" (Philippians 4:6-7). He graciously encourages us to talk to Him! "Pour out your heart before Him" (Psalm 62:8). Many psalms start out as surprisingly honest heartfelt laments. Then they end in hope and even thanksgiving! Yes, as hard as it might seem, thank Him for the trials, the struggles (Psalm 34:1). Why? It shows you believe He is good. You have faith in His power.

When conflict arises, remember a woman's "quiet spirit" is "precious in the sight of God" (I Peter 3:4). When I am tempted to blurt out, argue, or nag, I need to ask God to "keep watch over the door of my lips" (Psalm 141:3). Moses told the Israelites, "the LORD will fight for you while you keep silent" (Exodus 14:14). I love the whole story of the Passover, the Exodus, and the Red Sea crossing. These events are referred to many times throughout the rest of the Bible and remind me that God is able to deliver.

On the other hand, in certain cases, there are definitely times to speak up (Ecclesiastes 3:7; Esther 4:13-14). Unfortunately, the tendency for me is to not wait on His timing. When I do speak up, I need to say His Spirit-filled words. If I have a disagreement with my husband, I ask the LORD, "If He is wrong, change him."

And if my heart is right, I add, "If I am wrong, change me." Ultimately, I found that God is the only true tranquilizer!

## My Thoughts

---

---

---

---

---

---

---

---

---

---

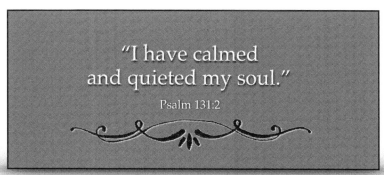

"I have calmed and quieted my soul."

Psalm 131:2

# 27

# A Place Where
# There Is No
# Loneliness

A Place Where
There Is No Loneliness

## Our Future Home

If our name is written in the Lamb's book of life, we will someday enter God's city, the New Jerusalem. The Bible gives a list of who will be there. We will see thousands upon thousands of angels, and come to "the general assembly and church of the firstborn who are enrolled in heaven, and to God, the Judge of all, and to the spirits of the righteous made perfect, and to Jesus" (Hebrews 12:22-24). God's city is well populated! And it's a place of countless happy reunions!

When Old Testament saints died, it was often said, "he was gathered unto his people" (Genesis 25:8). Some think this simply meant the body would be placed in the family tomb. However, Jacob "was gathered to his people," then embalmed 40 days, after which his body was brought to Canaan before being buried (Genesis 49:33, 50:1-12; Deuteronomy 34:4-6). Furthermore, Jesus said, "Regarding the resurrection of the dead, have you not read what was spoken to you by God: 'I am the God of Abraham, and the God of Isaac, and the God of Jacob'? He is not the God of the dead but of the living" (Matthew 22:31-32). The idea of heavenly reunions is not wishful thinking but God's plan!

He knows well that the heartbreak and pain of death is separation from those we love (John 11:32-26). God graciously paints a dramatic picture of parents being reunited with their children when Messiah comes to set up His kingdom. "Lift up your eyes round about and see; they all gather together, they come to you. Your sons will come from afar, and your daughters will be carried in the arms. Then you will see and be radiant, and your heart will thrill and rejoice" (Isaiah 60:4-5). King David trusted in the Lord for a blessed reunion when his infant son died. David was confident that he would see his son again. "I will go to him, but he will not return to me" (II Samuel 12:23). These saints of old were looking forward to living in "the city... whose architect and builder is God" (Hebrews 11:10). Someday when we come in to our Father's house, we will meet them and thousands of others. It will not be a lonely place!

## Our Home Today

A lot of people today are more alone than they ever intended to be. A TV or a pet can help, or even social media. But God knows we need the friendship and fellowship of other human beings. "God sets the lonely in families" (Psalm 68:6, NIV). He encourages us to reach out to others in all kinds of ways. For some, this comes naturally, but others have to make a conscious effort. Fellowship was a mark of the early church and they often took "their meals together" (Acts 2:42, 46). And as we think about reaching out, remember others who may be lonely. When we invite the needy, it's as though we are doing it to Christ (Matthew 25:35). The "one anothers" are all over the Bible! (See how many you can find!)

Most importantly we need to stay close to God. He doesn't move but we do. We are prone to wander. "He Himself has said, 'I will never desert you, nor will I ever forsake you'"(Hebrews 13:5). A Christian is never truly alone. "If anyone loves Me, he will keep My word; and My Father will love him, and We will come to him and make Our abode with him" (John 14:23).

# My Thoughts

"I will never desert you,
nor will I ever forsake you."

Hebrews 13:5

# A Place of
# Respect

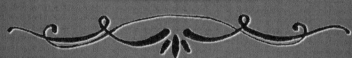

# A Place of Respect for Authority

## Our Future Home

Someday, when we dwell with our heavenly Father, we will give Him the respect He deserves. A stunning picture of this is when Jesus appeared to the apostle John. Jesus' "eyes were like a flame of fire...and His face was like the sun shining in its strength." John "fell at His feet like a dead man." But Jesus said, "Do not be afraid; I am the first and the last, and the living One; and I was dead, and behold, I am alive forevermore, and I have the keys of death and of Hades" (Revelation 1:14-18). What an extreme but appropriate example of respect toward the Lord God Almighty! He is the only One worthy of this awe. But here also is a beautiful example of kindness given. The One who embodies all authority says, "Do not be afraid" (Revelation 1:17).

## Our Home Today

In our culture today, many can hardly fathom what it is like to give respect to someone in authority. Even "Yes sir" and "yes ma'am" seem outdated. But true respect will show up in our attitude, our words and our actions. Early in my Christian walk when I was just starting to learn the Bible, I was taught an important lesson from an older woman. She was herself following guidance from the Lord: "Older women...encourage the young women to be... subject to their own husbands, so that the word of God will not be dishonored" (Titus

2:3-5). I saw from the Scriptures how critical it was to submit to God's plan for the family. God says that a wife ought to respect her husband (Ephesians 5:33). I learned that my attitude toward my husband actually showed that I was trusting in the Lord (I Peter 3:1-6). Not only this, but my children were watching. My example could help them in their obedience to God. And a husband's love toward his wife would help his children understand Christ's love. With kind leadership, he could show tenderness like Jesus showed John.

My husband and I found the following three verses in a bookstore. I put them in frames and hung them together on our wall to help us remember God's guidelines for the family. "Husbands, love your wives, just as Christ also loved the church and gave Himself up for her" (Ephesians 5:25). "Wives, be subject to your own husbands, as to the Lord" (Ephesians 5:22). And "Children, obey your parents in the Lord, for this is right" (Ephesians 6:1). An atmosphere of respect for authority was our goal, and with a lot of help from the Lord, we all tried to work at this throughout our family structure.

We also knew it was important to show respect for leaders outside our home such as pastors, teachers, policemen, and government. Inside our home our attitudes and conversations needed to show consistent respect for all those in authority. "Every person is to be in subjection to the governing authority. For there is no authority except from God" (Romans 13:1-5). Of course if at any time any exercise of authority is abused, we knew that our ultimate authority is the Lord. In that case "we must obey God rather than men" (Acts 5:27-29). Again, the Bible as a whole is a balanced guide. How thankful we all are that God not only teaches us how these important relationships are to function, but He promises to help us as we struggle to put these principles into practice.

## My Thoughts

_____

_____

_____

_____

_____

_____

_____

_____

_____

_____

_____

"Wives, be subject
to your own husbands,
as to the Lord."

Ephesians 5:22

#29

# A Place Where
# God Is Known

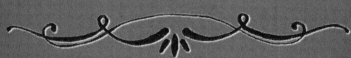

## A Place Where
# God Is Known

## Our Future Home

When we come to the very last book in the Bible, Jesus personally promises and exhorts: "Blessed is he who reads and those who hear the words of the prophecy, and heed the things which are written in it; for the time is near" (Revelation 1:3). We have seen how the book of Revelation is loaded with exciting promises about our future home. We have also harmonized these prophecies with many others throughout the whole Bible. Someday "the earth will be full of the knowledge of the LORD as the waters cover the sea" (Isaiah 11:9). That is the future of our world. That is the real goal. Some think the goal is to gain eternal life but Jesus said, "This is eternal life, that they may know You, the only true God, and Jesus Christ whom You have sent" (John 17:3). It's all about relationship. Since the Lord already knows us through and through, we need to make sure we know Him.

## Our Home Today

How do we do that? God has revealed Himself through His Word. He has not been silent! When our family first got in a Bible believing church, personal Bible reading was strongly encouraged. We are grateful that our children were still very young, so we learned and grew together. We were taught to study to show ourselves "approved to God as a workman who does not need to be ashamed, accurately handling the word of truth" (II Timothy 2:15).

An eighty-year-old woman taught me by her example. She had a notebook chock-full of notes, questions, and prayer requests. She read her Bible with pen in hand, an eager learner, a serious student of the Word. She encouraged me to be faithful to have a set time and place each day where I could get to know my God. With His help, I gradually made it a habit to do that.

I also understood how critical it was to train my children to come to know God. I knew that could only be through prayer and teaching the truths of His Word. He said, "These words, which I am commanding you today, shall be on your heart. You shall teach them diligently to your sons and shall talk of them when you sit in your house and when you walk by the way and when you lie down and when you rise up" (Deuteronomy 6:6-7). As a mother I had the opportunity to be the primary influence on a soul that was going to exist forever somewhere.

Years later, when I was a busy pastor's wife, homeschooling a large family, and rehabbing a house, my days were packed to the max! But my husband was working two jobs at the time, and I had more time with the children than he did. Each day I read to them from their Bible story book, but struggled to have my own Bible time too. I asked God to somehow help me be in my Bible. I decided to start reading to them through the Bible directly. Inspired by Deuteronomy 6:20 I told them, "You can interrupt at any time with any question as long as it pertains to the Bible." Their questions amazed me. Their understanding grew and was a total joy. We had great discussions that sometimes went on for over an hour! Then I realized they were getting out of Math and English! It's that balance thing!

One by one they came to know God and accept His gift of salvation. I saw His Spirit work through His Word. And that was the goal!

## My Thoughts

_____

_____

_____

_____

_____

_____

_____

_____

_____

_____

"This is eternal life,
that they may know You,
the only true God, and Jesus Christ
whom You have sent."

John 17:3

#30

A Place
For
You

## Our Future Home

This world is full of broken families, broken people, and broken hearts. Those who have trusted God's Messiah, Jesus, have "an inheritance which is imperishable and undefiled and will not fade away, reserved in heaven for you" (I Peter 1:4). This is one home that is not broken, and will never be broken!

Just imagine what it will be like to hear King Jesus say, "Come, you who are blessed of My Father, inherit the kingdom prepared for you from the foundation of the world" (Matthew 25:34). Jesus comforted His followers with these words, "Do not let your heart be troubled; believe in God, believe also in Me. In My Father's house are many dwelling places; if it were not so, I would have told you; for I go to prepare a place for you. If I go and prepare a place for you, I will come again and receive you to Myself, that where I am, there you may be also" (John 14:2-3). The Father's house that has many dwelling places sounds like what Ezekiel described: a single structure that is a city! (Ezekiel 40:2) And Ezekiel said, "The name of the city from that day shall be 'The LORD is there'" (Ezekiel 48:35). This is personal. It's prepared for you and reserved for you! You don't want to miss this!

## Our Home Today

That night when Jesus talked to His followers about His Father's house, He added, "'And you know the way where I am going.' Thomas said to Him, 'Lord, we do not know where You are going, how do we know the way?' Jesus said to him, 'I am the way, and the truth, and the life; no one comes to the Father but through Me" (John 14:4-6).

The life that Jesus is talking about is eternal life. If you are not sure that you have eternal life, you can know and be sure. "These things I have written to you who believe in the name of the Son of God, so that you may **know** that you have eternal life" (I John 5:13). You need to first acknowledge that you have sinned and understand that sin separates you from God. "For the wages of sin is death" (Romans 6:23). That is the bad news. The good news is that Jesus paid the penalty for your sin. "God demonstrates His own love toward us, in that while we were yet sinners, Christ died for us" (Romans 5:8). If you understand that and "confess with your mouth Jesus as Lord, and believe in your heart that God raised Him from the dead, you will be saved; for with the heart a person believes, resulting in righteousness, and with the mouth he confesses, resulting in salvation…for 'Whoever will call on the name of the LORD will be saved'" (Romans 10:9-13).

Many years ago, I read those very same Bible verses in a little gospel tract. I was alone in my bedroom, understood the words, believed them, and prayed to ask Jesus to be my Savior. If you have never done that, you can do that right now. You can pray something like this:

Dear God, I have sinned against You. Please forgive my sins and allow Jesus' sacrifice to count as payment for my sin. Thank You for Your great provision. Thank You for saving me.

If you believe this and have prayed this prayer, then you will inherit God's Kingdom promises. Tell your family! "Let your light so shine…to all that are in the house" (Matthew 5:15-16). I would love to hear about it too! (scottandjanetwillis@gmail.com)

# My Thoughts

_____

_____

_____

_____

_____

_____

_____

_____

_____

_____

_____

_____

"In My Father's house
are many dwelling places...
I go to prepare a place for you."

John 14:2

## About the Photos:

1 -  Note holder made by Joe (age 5)
2 -  My mom holding me (1947)
3 -  Amy with my first grandchild, Sara,
       and me with my ninth child, Peter
5 -  Ben hugging Elizabeth
8 -  Elizabeth helping in the kitchen
10 - Amy with my mother-in-law, Clare
12 - Ben, Joe, Sam, and Hank
       come in after Elizabeth's birth
14 - Hank with his paper crown
15 - Grandson Seth holding his new little sister,
       Eliza
16 - My family around the piano
18 - Granddaughter Eliza imitating her mom, Amy
23 - Sam having fun!
25 - Dan and his sons with Grandpa Scott
27 - Dan and Toby home from college
       with Ben, Joe, Sam, and Hank
29 - Bible time with Ben, Joe, Sam, and Hank